A Patrick Lose CHRISTMAS

Whimsical
Projects
to Deck
the Halls

C&T PUBLISHING

Text copyright © 2008 by Patrick Lose

Artwork copyright © 2008 by C&T Publishing, Inc.

Publisher: **Amy Marson**

Creative Director: **Gailen Runge**

Acquisitions Editor: **Jan Grigsby**

Editor: **Gailen Runge**

Technical Editors: **Carolyn Aune, Teresa Stroin, and Joyce Lytle**

Copyeditor/Proofreader: **Wordfirm Inc.**

Cover Designer/Design Director: **Kristen Yenche**

Book Designer/Junior Designer: **Kerry Graham**

Production Coordinator: **Zinnia Heinzmann**

Illustrator: **Tim Manibusan**

Photography by Luke Mulks and Diane Pedersen of C&T Publishing unless
otherwise noted

Published by C&T Publishing, Inc., P.O. Box 1456, Lafayette, CA 94549

Library of Congress Cataloging-in-Publication Data

Lose, Patrick.

A Patrick Lose Christmas : whimsical projects to deck the halls / Patrick Lose.

p. cm.

Summary: "12 projects for Christmas in Patrick Lose's inimitable style. Book includes
instructions for quilts, tablerunners, and pillows."--Provided by publisher.

ISBN 978-1-57120-339-7 (paper trade : alk. paper)

1. Christmas decorations. 2. Textile crafts. I. Title.

TT900.C4L67 2008

745.594'12--dc22

Printed in China

10 9 8 7 6 5 4 3 2 1

Dedication

This book is dedicated to the

loving memory of my parents,

Joan and John Lose. I'm

thankful for the many merry

Christmases they gave me.

Table of Contents

Ho Ho Ho

Introduction

Charles Dickens wrote, "I will honor Christmas in my heart and try to keep it all the year." That's a great sentiment that I try to live by myself. I could work on Christmas designs every day of the year. I never get tired of them. Sometimes, in the Arizona desert heat, I have to admit it's a little harder to muster the motivation. But it always comes in time.

Ever since I was a kid, I've enjoyed making Christmas-themed projects. I think the reason that the ideas come so easily to me now is that I enjoyed Christmas so much growing up. I have a vast collection of cherished memories from which to draw. Like Dickens, my parents knew how to honor and keep Christmas, and they set a great example for their children and grandchildren. I consider myself lucky for that.

I love traditional themes at Christmas, but with this book, I wanted to convey the lighter side and offer some whimsical and jolly projects. I hope you enjoy making them as much as I enjoyed designing them.

Another of my favorite Christmas sentiments is from Thomas Tusser: "At Christmas play and make good cheer, for Christmas comes but once a year." I can definitely live up to that one, and I hope this book helps you to do the same. Enjoy!

Cheers,

Patrick

Caramel Christmas Mix

2-lb bag brown sugar
1 lb butter (not margarine)
1 C light corn syrup
2 T pure vanilla extract
1 box Rice Chex
1 box Corn Chex
1 box Crispex
2 C pecan pieces

Bring first 3 ingredients to a boil. Once boiling, stir constantly for 5 minutes. Remove from heat and stir in vanilla. Pour over cereal and pecans, stirring to coat. Put in pans and bake at 200 degrees for one hour. Remove from oven and pour out onto wax paper or foil to cool.

A word to the wise: Do not allow children to eat this near bedtime.

Patrick Lose

Holiday Cheer

About ten years ago, at a friend's Christmas get-together, I spent the evening hovering over a bowl of snack mix that I just couldn't stop eating. This was unusual for me, and I was surprised that I had even tried it. It wasn't the kind of thing I usually go for. But I found myself completely hooked. When it was time to go, I had a doggy bag of it in my hands. If memory serves, it was gone by the time I got home. The next day I tracked down my friend and asked for the recipe. There's no telling what might have happened if he hadn't given it to me.

Years later, it's still usually the first thing I make to have around during the holidays. And I always offer the recipe to anyone I find hovering over the bowl at my parties too. So, here it is for any of you who haven't already gotten it from one of your more "addiction enabling" friends. *Enjoy!* *

* **Disclaimer:** *Patrick Lose is not responsible for the intrinsic weight gains, sugar buzzes, gluttony, or cloying addictions resulting from the consumption of this treat. Eat at your own risk.*

General Instructions

As tempting as it may be to jump right into your project, read the instructions thoroughly before you begin. All piecing for the projects in *A Patrick Lose Christmas* are sewn using a ¼″ seam allowance and are stitched with the fabrics placed right sides together.

Tools

Make sure you have all the necessary tools at hand before you start cutting and stitching up a storm. It's easy to let your excitement for the project get the best of you, but then you'll be off to the quilt shop to buy more fabric or to hunt for a seam ripper. Following is a list of helpful tools that will make your stitching easier.

- Rotary cutter and cutting mat
- Transparent acrylic gridded ruler
- Sewing machine in good working order capable of doing a narrow zigzag or satin stitch
- Paper scissors
- Fabric scissors
- Lightbox (or large window)
- Sewing machine needles, size 80/12 universal
- Threads, 100% cotton

- Iron and ironing board
- Pressing paper or cloth (to avoid a messy iron)
- Walking foot for machine quilting
- Darning foot for free-motion quilting
- Safety pins
- Fusible web
- Lightweight tear-away stabilizer
- Permanent black marker with a fine tip for marking pattern pieces
- Fabric markers for adding facial details and titles

Fabrics

I don't prewash my fabrics for quilting. This is my personal preference, and I have never had a problem with colors bleeding. If I do wash the finished piece, the minimal shrinkage creates a slightly puckered quilt with a softer look and feel. Some people always prewash, and that is perfectly fine. Just be sure that if you prewash, you use warm water to allow the fabric to shrink as much as it is going to. Tumble dry the fabric and remove from the dryer when it is still slightly damp. Always iron the fabric before measuring and cutting. Do not use starch on fabrics that will be used for appliqué pieces. It could make the fabric difficult to fuse.

It is extremely important to measure and cut your fabrics accurately and to stitch using an exact $1/4''$ seam allowance. I am certain you'll be proud of your finished piece if you follow these simple rules.

Appliqué

The appliqué projects in this book use a fusible-adhesive appliqué method, and the appliqués are outlined using a machine satin or zigzag stitch. In this book, all the patterns for appliqué are printed actual size and are reversed for tracing onto paper-backed fusible adhesive. Be sure to use a lightweight paper-backed fusible adhesive that is suitable for sewing. Should you wish to do hand appliqué (knock yourself out), you'll need to trace the printed patterns in mirror image and add seam allowances to them. For a couple of the projects, I have used a permanent black fabric marker to color the pupils of the eyes. To keep the marker from bleeding, blow on the area as you are marking it.

Fusible Appliqué Preparations

Patterns are printed actual size and are reversed for tracing onto fusible adhesive. If necessary when tracing, join the pieces as indicated on the pattern.

1 Lay the fusible adhesive, paper side up, over each pattern piece and use a pencil to trace the shape onto the paper side. Write the pattern name, piece number, and fabric color on each piece as you trace it.

Note: In places where the pieces butt one another, overlapping them helps to keep them from gapping. Either you can cut the pieces exact and then overlap by a hair, or (particularly if you are new to satin stitching) you can add approximately $1/16''$ to the underneath piece. Please note that the latter method will add some bulk to your project.

2 Be sure to trace any appliqué placement lines or detail stitching lines using a fabric pencil or permanent marker.

3 Use paper-cutting scissors to roughly cut all the pieces approximately $1/4''$ outside the traced lines.

4 Following the manufacturer's instructions for the fusible adhesive, fuse the traced pattern piece onto the wrong side of the fabric listed on each template.

5 Cut out the pieces along the traced lines.

6 Transfer any placement and stitching lines to the right side of the fabric using a lightbox and a pencil.

Tip: If the project includes light-colored pieces that will be placed on top of a dark layer or background, fuse two layers of the light fabric together to prevent color show-through. Then fuse the traced pattern to the back of the bottom light layer.

Tip: Be sure to layer and arrange all the pieces on the background in an arrangement you like before fusing any of them.

Layering and Quilting

I like to use a single layer of thin cotton batting such as Warm & Natural. Cut your backing fabric and batting to measure 2″ to 3″ larger than your quilt top on all sides. (I allow 2″ extra on all sides for small projects and 3″ extra on all sides for the larger projects.) Sandwich the batting between the quilt top and the backing, wrong sides together, and baste through all layers, smoothing the quilt top outward from the center. You can also use safety pins spaced 4″ to 6″ apart.

All the quilting in this book was done by machine. I use a walking foot for straight-line quilting. For free-motion or stipple quilting, I use a darning foot and lower the feed dogs on my machine. You can also quilt by hand if you'd like; hand quilting would be a beautiful addition to the look of these pieces. Quilt as desired or refer to the photos and quilting suggestions that are included with each project. A Chaco Liner is great for marking quilting lines if you are not comfortable eyeballing them, and the chalk lines can be easily brushed away. When quilting appliqué projects, be sure to quilt around the appliqué shapes.

Binding

The instructions for each project give you the amount of binding necessary to finish your quilt project.

1 Cut 2⅛″-wide strips selvage to selvage using a rotary cutter, a mat, and a transparent acrylic gridded ruler. These strips will measure 40″–44″ long after you have straightened your fabric and cut off the selvages.

2 Use diagonal seams to join binding strips. Trim the seam allowances and press the seams open.

Stitch

3 Fold the completed binding strip in half length-wise with the wrong sides together. Press.

4 Place the folded binding strip on the right edge of the quilt top, beginning in the center of the edge and aligning the raw edges of the quilt and the binding. Fold over the beginning of the binding strip about ½″. Stitch through all the layers using a ¼″ seam allowance. Stop stitching ¼″ from the corner. Backstitch at least 2 stitches, remove the quilt from the machine, and clip the threads.

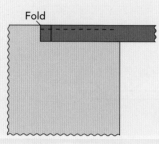

Fold

5 Fold up the binding and crease the fold with your fingers.

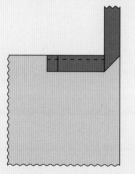

6 Holding the creased fold in place, fold the binding down and align the raw edges with the next side of the quilt. Start stitching again at the corner, through all the layers. Stitch around the entire quilt, treating each corner as you did the first.

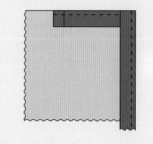

7 When you return to where you started, stitch the binding beyond the fold you made in the strip at the beginning. Backstitch at least 2 stitches and clip the threads. Cut off the excess batting and backing fabric so that all the layers are even.

8 Turn the binding over the quilt edge, aligning the fold of the binding with the machine stitching you just finished. You can pin the binding in place, but I like to use those funny little hair clips that bend and then snap closed; they work great and don't prick your fingers or get stuck in the carpet. You can find them at most variety stores and drugstores, and fabric stores often carry them in their quilting notions sec-tion. Hand sew the binding onto the backing, making sure you cover the machine stitching. Miter the cor-ners on the back side of the quilt also, stitching the miter fold in place if necessary.

Be sure to display your work of art in a conspicuous place where it is most likely to prompt compliments, but keep in mind that direct sunlight will fade fabric more quickly than you might think. Remember that because these projects are seasonal, you probably won't display them year-round. If you store them in cotton casings, not plastic, they should last to grace your home for many merry holiday seasons.

Christmastime
Bed Quilt

I like the way that the colors and the playful design of the pinwheels made me instantly think of the Christmas season. Simply reduce the number of blocks to create a throw or a quilt for a child's bed.

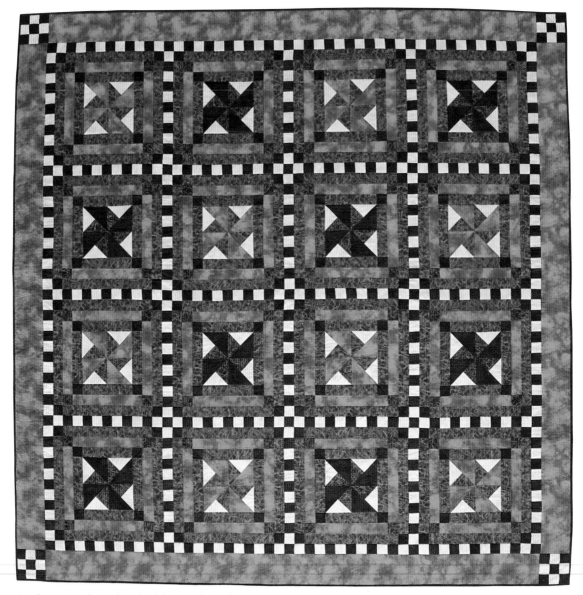

Quilt top made and quilted by: *Heidi Pridemore and The Whimsical Workshop*

Finished Block: 22″ × 22″   Finished Quilt: 110″ × 110″

Fabric and Supplies

- **Green 1:** 3¾ yards for Pinwheels and block borders 1 and 3

- **Green 2:** 4⅜ yards for Pinwheels, block border 2, and outer border

- **Cherry 1:** 11 yards (1 yard for Pinwheels and block border 2 cornerstones and 10 yards for backing)

- **Cherry 2:** 3⅜ yards (2½ yards for Pinwheels, checkerboard sashing, checkerboard connectors, outer-border checkerboard corners, and block borders 1 and 3 cornerstones and ⅞ yard for binding)

- **Ivory:** 2¼ yards for Pinwheels, checkerboard sashing, and outer-border checkerboard corners

- **Thin cotton batting:** 116″ × 116″

Cutting Fabrics

Use a rotary cutter, mat, and ruler to cut the following pieces from the width of the fabric.

Tip: Lightly starch each pinwheel fabric listed below. Starching the fabric will make working with the bias triangles easier because they will be less likely to stretch.

From Green 1:

Cut 2 strips 6¼″ × width of fabric. Subcut into 8 squares 6¼″ × 6¼″. Cut each square twice on the diagonal to make 32 triangles (1).

Cut 4 strips 10½″ × width of fabric. Subcut into 64 strips 2½″ × 10½″ for block border 1.

Cut 4 strips 18½″ × width of fabric. Subcut into 64 strips 2½″ × 18½″ for block border 3.

From Green 2:

Cut 3 strips 5⅞″ × width of fabric. Subcut into 16 squares 5⅞″ × 5⅞″. Cut each square on one diagonal to make 32 triangles (3).

Cut 4 strips 14½″ × width of fabric. Subcut into 64 strips 2½″ × 14½″ for block border 2.

Cut 10 strips 6½″ × width of fabric. Piece the strips together end to end as necessary and cut into 4 strips 6½″ × 98½″ for the outer border.

From Cherry 1:

Cut 2 strips 6¼″ × width of fabric. Subcut into 8 squares 6¼″ × 6¼″. Cut each square twice on the diagonal to make 32 triangles (1).

Cut 4 strips 2½″ × width of fabric. Subcut into 64 squares 2½″ × 2½″ for block border 2 cornerstones.

Cut 3 sections 116″ from the length of the fabric. Sew the sections together to make 1 square 116″ × 116″ for the backing.

From Cherry 2:

Cut 3 strips 5⅞″ × width of fabric. Subcut into 16 squares 5⅞″ × 5⅞″. Cut each square on one diagonal to make 32 triangles (3).

Cut 11 strips 2½″ × width of fabric. Subcut into 173 squares 2½″ × 2½″ for the checkerboard connectors, outer-border checkerboard corners, and block borders 1 and 3 cornerstones.

Cut 15 strips 2½″ × width of fabric for the checkerboard sashing.

Cut 13 strips 2⅛″ × width of fabric for the binding.

From Ivory:

Cut 3 strips 6¼″ × width of fabric. Subcut into 16 squares 6¼″ × 6¼″. Cut each square twice on one diagonal to make 64 triangles (2).

Cut 18 strips 2½″ × width of fabric for the checkerboard sashing.

Cut 1 strip 2½″ × width of fabric. Subcut into 16 squares 2½″ × 2½″ for the outer-border checkerboard corners.

Block Assembly

1 Place a green 1 triangle (1) on an ivory triangle (2) right sides together. Sew down the right short side of the triangles as shown. Press the seam toward the green 1 fabric to make a green unit A section. Repeat to make 32 green 1 unit A sections total.

Make 32.

2 Repeat Step 1 with 32 cherry 1 triangles (1) and 32 ivory triangles (2) to make 32 cherry unit A sections total.

Make 32.

3 Place a green 2 triangle (3) on top of a green unit A section from Step 1 right sides together, aligning the edges of the triangles. Sew the triangles together down the long sides of the triangles to make a green triangle block. Press the seam toward the green fabric. The block should measure 5½″ × 5½″ (unfinished). Make 32 green triangle blocks total.

Make 32.

4 Repeat Step 3 with the cherry unit A sections and 32 cherry 2 triangles (3) to make 32 red triangle blocks total.

Make 32.

5 Following the block center layout diagrams, below, sew 4 green triangle blocks together to make 8 green block centers. Sew 4 red triangle blocks together to make 8 red block centers. Press. Each block center should measure 10½″ × 10½″ (unfinished).

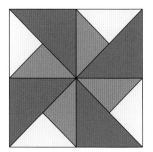

Make 8.

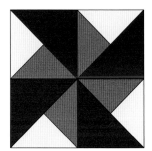

Make 8.

6 Following the block layout diagrams, at right, sew a 2½″ × 10½″ green 1 strip to each side of the 16 block centers. Press the seams toward the strips.

7 Sew a 2½″ × 2½″ cherry 2 square to each of the remaining 2½″ × 10½″ green 1 strips. Press the seams toward the strips. Sew a strip to the top and bottom of each block center. Press the seams toward the outer strips.

8 Sew a 2½″ × 14½″ green 2 strip to each side of the block centers. Press the seams toward the outer strips.

9 Sew a 2½″ cherry 1 square to each end of the remaining 2½″ × 14½″ green 2 strips. Press the seams toward the strips. Sew the strips to the top and bottom of the block centers. Press the seams toward the outer strips.

10 Sew a 2½″ × 18½″ green 1 strip to each side of the block centers. Press the seams toward the outer strips.

11 Sew a 2½″ × 2½″ cherry 2 square to each end of the remaining 2½″ × 18½″ green 1 strips. Press the seams toward the strips. Sew the strips to the top and bottom of the block centers. Press. The blocks should measure 22½″ × 22½″ (unfinished).

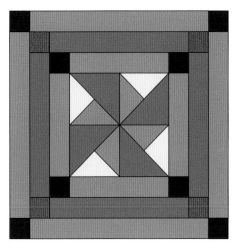

Make 8.

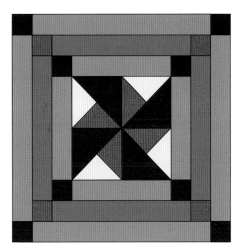

Make 8.

Checkerboard Sashing and Cornerstone Assembly

1 Sew together 6 ivory strips $2\frac{1}{2}'' \times$ width of fabric lengthwise with 5 cherry 2 strips $2\frac{1}{2}'' \times$ width of fabric, alternating the strips to make 1 sashing strip set. Press the seams toward the cherry strips. Repeat to make 3 sashing strip sets total.

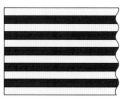

Make 3.

2 Cut 40 sashing segments $2\frac{1}{2}''$ wide from the sashing strip sets.

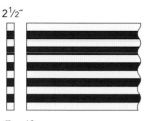

2½"

Cut 40.

3 Make the horizontal sashing strips: starting and ending with 1 cherry 2 square $2\frac{1}{2}'' \times 2\frac{1}{2}''$, sew together 4 sashing segments $2\frac{1}{2}''$ wide from Step 2 and 5 cherry 1 squares $2\frac{1}{2}'' \times 2\frac{1}{2}''$, alternating the segments and the squares, to make a horizontal sashing strip. Make 5 horizontal sashing strips.

■▬■▬■▬■▬■

Make 5.

4 To make the checkerboard cornerstones, follow the cornerstone layout diagram, below, and alternate 1 cherry 1 square $2\frac{1}{2}'' \times 2\frac{1}{2}''$ with 1 ivory square $2\frac{1}{2}'' \times 2\frac{1}{2}''$ to make the rows of the checkerboard square. Press the seams toward the cherry squares.

5 Sew the rows together to make 1 checkerboard square. Press the seams toward the top and bottom rows. Repeat to make 4 checkerboard cornerstones total. Set aside.

Make 4.

Quilt Top Assembly

1. Refer to the quilt photo for block center color placement when sewing the rows together. Starting and ending with a sashing segment, sew together 5 sashing segments, 2 blocks with a green center, and 2 blocks with a cherry center to make 1 row. Press. Make 4 block rows total.

2. Refer to the diagram, at left, for color placement when sewing the rows together. Starting and ending with a horizontal sashing strip, sew together the 4 block rows and 5 horizontal sashing strips to make the quilt top. Press.

3. Sew a green 2 outer-border strip $6\frac{1}{2}'' \times 98\frac{1}{2}''$ to each side of the quilt top. Press the seams toward the border.

4. Sew 1 checkerboard cornerstone to each end of the remaining green 2 outer-border strips $6\frac{1}{2}'' \times 98\frac{1}{2}''$. Press the seams toward the border strips. Sew the strips to the top and bottom of the quilt top. Press.

Quilting

Refer to Layering and Quilting (page 8) and Binding (page 8–9).

1. Sandwich the batting between the quilt top and backing, wrong sides together, smoothing the quilt top outward from the center. Baste as desired.

2. Quilt as desired.

3. Bind the quilt.

Christmas Cabin
Table Runner

The table is often the gathering place for the holidays. This festively colored runner is great by itself or beneath your favorite holiday centerpiece.

Quilt top made and quilted by: *Heidi Pridemore and The Whimsical Workshop*

Finished Block: 9½″ × 9½″   Finished Quilt: 14½″ × 44½″

Fabric and Supplies

- **Green 1:** ⅝ yard (¼ yard for Log Cabin blocks and outer-border cornerstones and ⅜ yard for binding)

- **Green 2:** 1¾ yards (¼ yard for Log Cabin blocks and 1½ yards for backing)

- **Cherry 1:** ⅝ yard for Log Cabin blocks and outer border

- **Cherry 2:** ¼ yard for Log Cabin blocks

- **Ivory:** ⅜ yard for checkerboard sashing

- **Black:** ⅜ yard for checkerboard sashing

- **Thin cotton batting:** 19″ × 49″

Cutting Fabrics

Use a rotary cutter, mat, and ruler to cut the following pieces from the width of the fabric.

From Green 1:

Cut 6 strips 1″ × width of fabric. Subcut into 16 strips 1″ × 2″, 16 strips 1″ × 2½″, 16 strips 1″ × 4″, and 16 strips 1″ × 4½″.

Cut 1 strip 2½″ × width of fabric. Subcut into 4 squares 2½″ × 2½″ for outer-border cornerstones.

Cut 4 strips 2⅛″ × width of fabric for the binding.

From Green 2:

Cut 4 strips 1″ × width of fabric. Subcut into 16 squares 1″ × 1″, 16 strips 1″ × 1½″, 16 strips 1″ × 3″, and 16 strips 1″ × 3½″.

Cut a 19″ × 49″ piece for backing.

From Cherry 1:

Cut 7 strips 1″ × width of fabric. Subcut into 16 squares 1″ × 1″, 16 strips 1″ × 2½″, 16 strips 1″ × 3″, 16 strips 1″ × 4½″, and 16 strips 1″ × 5″.

Cut 3 strips 2½″ × width of fabric. Subcut into 2 strips 2½″ × 41″ and 2 strips 2½″ × 11″ for the outer border.

From Cherry 2:

Cut 5 strips 1″ × width of fabric. Subcut into 16 strips 1″ × 1½″, 16 strips 1″ × 2″, 16 strips 1″ × 3½″, and 16 strips 1″ × 4″.

From Ivory:

Cut 5 strips 1″ × width of fabric. Subcut into 10 strips 1″ × 21″ for the checkerboard sashing.

From Black:

Cut 5 strips 1″ × width of fabric. Subcut 4 strips into 8 strips 1″ × 21″ for the checkerboard sashing; subcut 1 strip into 27 squares 1″ × 1″.

Checkerboard Sashing Assembly

1 Sew together 5 ivory strips 1″ × 21″ with 4 black strips 1″ × 21″, alternating the strips to make 1 sashing strip set. Press the seams toward the darker strips. Repeat to make 2 sashing strip sets total.

Make 2.

2 Cut 42 sashing segments 1″ wide from the sashing strip sets.

Cut 42.

3 To make the horizontal sashing strips, sew together 8 sashing segments alternating with 9 black squares 1″ × 1″, starting and ending with a black square. Press the seams toward the black squares. Repeat to make 2 horizontal sashing strips total.

Make 2.

4 To make the vertical sashing strips and block center strips, sew a 1″ × 5″ sashing segment to each side of a 1″ × 1″ black square. Press the seams toward the black square. Repeat to make 5 vertical sashing strips and 4 block sashing strips total.

Make 9.

Block Assembly

1 Sew a 1″ × 1″ green 2 square to the left side of a 1″ × 1″ cherry 1 square to make the block center. Press the seam toward the green square.

2 Turn the block center counterclockwise and add a 1″ × 1½″ green 2 strip. Press the seam toward the 1″ × 1½″ strip.

3 Referring to the Log Cabin layout diagram, below, continue to add strips by turning the unit counter-clockwise and sewing on the next strip. Always press the seam toward the newly added strip. Make 16 Log Cabin units 5″ × 5″ (unfinished) total.

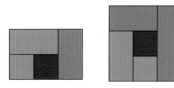

Turn counterclockwise to add next strip.

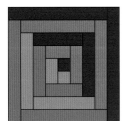

Make 16.

4 Sew a Log Cabin unit to each side of a sashing segment to make a block half. Press the seams toward the Log Cabin units. Repeat to make 8 block halves total.

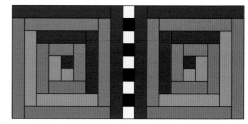

Make 8.

5 Sew a block half to the top and bottom of 1 block sashing strip to make 1 block 10″ × 10″ (unfinished). Press the seams toward the block halves. Repeat to make 4 blocks total.

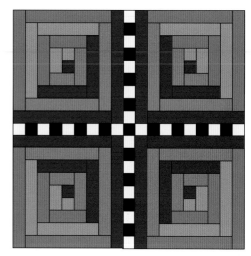

Make 4.

Quilt Top Assembly

1. Starting with a block sashing strip and alternating with the blocks, sew together 4 blocks and the 5 remaining block sashing strips. Press the seams toward the blocks.

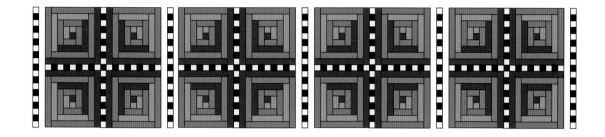

2. Sew 1 horizontal sashing strip to the top and bottom of the quilt top. Press the seams toward the quilt top.

3. Sew a 2½″ × 11″ cherry strip to each side of the quilt top. Press the seams toward the strips.

4. Sew a 2½″ × 2½″ green square to each end of the 2 cherry strips 2½″ × 41″. Press the seams toward the strips.

5. Sew the strips to the top and bottom of the quilt top. Press the seams toward the strips.

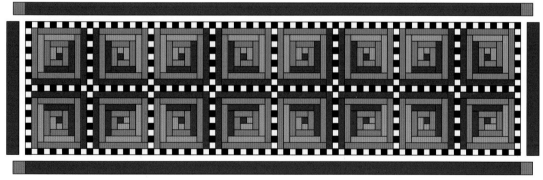

Quilting

Refer to Layering and Quilting (page 8) and Binding (pages 8–9).

1. Sandwich the batting between the quilt top and backing, wrong sides together, smoothing the quilt top outward from the center. Baste as desired.

2. Quilt as desired.

3. Bind the quilt.

Happy Holidays

*W*hen his work's all done for another year, Santa takes a well-deserved break on an icy lake.

Quilt top made and quilted by: *Heidi Pridemore and The Whimsical Workshop*
Finished Quilt: 30″ × 34″ without banner   Banner: 6″ × 35″

Fabric and Supplies

- **Powder blue:** ¼ yard for ice

- **Sky blue:** ⅞ yard for sky

- **Green 1:** ⅝ yard (¼ for checkerboard border, trees, and Santa's mitten and ⅜ yard for binding)

- **Green 2:** 1¼ yards (¼ yard for checkerboard border and trees and 1 yard for backing)

- **Cherry:** 1 yard for banner, banner binding, and Santa's outfit

- **Snow:** ⅜ yard for hills, snowflakes, and Santa's accents

- **Nectar:** ⅛ yard for Santa's belt buckle, buttons, and skate bands

- **Black:** ⅛ yard for Santa's belt and skate boots

- **Dove:** 5″ × 5″ square for Santa's skates

- **Flesh:** 3″ × 3″ square for Santa's face

- **Blush:** 3″ × 3″ square for Santa's lip

- **Thin cotton batting:** 36″ × 40″ for quilt and 9″ × 40″ for banner

- **18″-wide lightweight paper-backed fusible adhesive:** 1½ yards

- **12″-wide tear-away stabilizer:** 3 yards

- **Black and white threads for satin stitching**

- **Permanent marker**

- **Fabric pencil**

Fusible Appliqué Preparations

All appliqué pattern pieces are on page 1 of the pullout. They are printed actual size and are reversed for tracing onto fusible adhesive. Trace the number of pieces indicated on the pattern. Refer to Appliqué (page 7) for instructions.

Cutting Fabrics

Use a rotary cutter, mat, and ruler to cut the following pieces from the width of the fabric.

From Powder Blue:

Cut 1 strip $6\frac{1}{2}'' \times 26\frac{1}{2}''$ for the ice.

From Sky Blue:

Cut 1 rectangle $24\frac{1}{2}'' \times 26\frac{1}{2}''$ for the sky.

From Green 1:

Cut 2 strips $2\frac{1}{2}'' \times$ width of fabric. Subcut into 30 squares $2\frac{1}{2}'' \times 2\frac{1}{2}''$ for the checkerboard border.

Cut 4 strips $2\frac{1}{8}'' \times$ width of fabric for the quilt binding.

See appliqué instructions, page 22, to make the trees (3 and 4) and Santa's mitten (15).

From Green 2:

Cut 2 strips $2\frac{1}{2}'' \times$ width of fabric. Subcut into 30 squares $2\frac{1}{2}'' \times 2\frac{1}{2}''$ for the checkerboard border.

Cut $36'' \times 40''$ piece for backing.

See appliqué instructions to make the trees (3 and 4).

From Cherry:

Cut 2 strips $9'' \times 40''$ for the banner (25, Parts A and B).

Cut 3 strips $2\frac{1}{8}'' \times$ width of fabric for the banner binding.

See appliqué instructions to make Santa's outfit (5, 9, 11, 17, and 18).

From Snow:

See appliqué instructions to make Santa's accents (6, 7, 14, 16, and 19), the hills (1 and 2), and the snowflakes (13).

From Nectar:

See appliqué instructions to make Santa's belt buckle (12), buttons (13), and skate bands (21 and 22).

From Black:

See appliqué instructions to make Santa's belt (10) and skate boots (20).

From Dove:

See appliqué instructions to make skate blades (23).

From Flesh:

See appliqué instructions to make Santa's face (8).

From Blush:

See appliqué instructions to make Santa's lip (24).

Quilt Top Assembly

Note: Assemble the quilt top before positioning and fusing the appliqués to the quilt top.

1. Sew the $6\frac{1}{2}'' \times 26\frac{1}{2}''$ powder blue strip to the bottom of the $24\frac{1}{2}'' \times 26\frac{1}{2}''$ sky blue piece to make the background. Press the seam open.

2. Referring to the quilt photo and illustration for placement, remove the paper backing from the hill appliqué pieces (1 and 2) and position them on the background. Fuse the hill pieces in place.

3. Starting and ending with a green 1 square, sew together 8 green 1 squares $2\frac{1}{2}'' \times 2\frac{1}{2}''$ and 7 green 2 squares $2\frac{1}{2}'' \times 2\frac{1}{2}''$ to make a side border. Press. Repeat to make 2 side borders total.

4. Sew the side borders to the background from Step 1. Press the seams toward the borders.

5 Starting and ending with a green 2 square, sew together 8 green 2 squares 2½″ × 2½″ and 7 green 1 squares 2½″ × 2½″ to make the top border. Press. Repeat to make the bottom border.

6 Sew the top and bottom borders to the quilt top. Press the seams toward the borders.

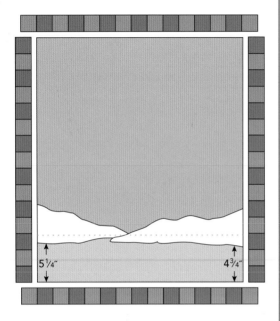

7 Referring to the quilt photo and illustration for placement, remove the paper backing from all the remaining appliqué pieces and position them on the quilt top, overlapping pieces as necessary.

8 When you are satisfied with the placement, fuse the pieces into place, smoothing the larger pieces as you proceed.

Satin Stitch Appliqué

Use a tear-away stabilizer on the wrong side of the background fabric. With thread suitable for machine appliqué, satin stitch around the appliqué pieces and any detail stitching lines. To satin stitch, use a fairly narrow zigzag stitch and keep your stitch length as short as possible. Stitch over the raw edges of the fused appliqué pieces so that none of the raw edges show. Work outward from the center and smooth the fabric as you proceed.

1 Using black thread, satin stitch the curl on the skates, the buttonholes and button threads, Santa's eyes and nose, the lines for Santa's mustache and hat, the accent lines on Santa's outfit, boot cuffs, and belt buckle, the lines around the hat pom-pom, and the tree trunks.

2 Using white thread, satin stitch around the snowflakes.

3 If you like, brush a little blush onto Santa's cheeks.

4 Fill in the mouth and eyes with permanent marker.

Banner Assembly

1 Using a lightbox and a fabric pencil, trace the lettering and accent lines for the banner onto a 9″ × 40″ cherry strip.

2 Put 1 batting strip 9″ × 40″ and 2 cherry strips 9″ × 40″ wrong sides together with the batting sandwiched between the cherry strips.

3 Quilt the lettering and accent lines for the banner following the drawn lines.

4 Piece together and trace the banner template pattern (25, Parts A and B) found on the pullout onto the top strip. Cut out the 3 layers to make the banner quilt sandwich.

5 Refer to Binding (pages 8–9) to add the cherry binding strips to finish the banner.

Quilting

Refer to Layering and Quilting (page 8) and Binding (pages 8–9).

1 Sandwich the batting between the quilt top and backing, wrong sides together, smoothing the quilt top outward from the center. Baste as desired.

2 Using monofilament thread, stitch around the outside of all the satin stitched details and shapes.

3 Using a walking foot and matching thread, stitch in-the-ditch between the border and background square.

4 Using a darning foot, with the machine feed dogs lowered, quilt the background with matching thread and a meandering stitch.

5 Bind the quilt.

Adding the Banner to the Quilt

To permanently attach the banner to the quilt, use a walking foot and matching thread to quilt the banner to the quilt top along the binding lines. Tack the top curve of the banner to the quilt using a whipstitch on the back side of the banner.

Ho! Ho! Ho!

J olly Old St. Nick lives up to his name in this wall quilt displaying the colors of Christmas.

Quilt top made and quilted by: *Heidi Pridemore and The Whimsical Workshop*

Finished Quilt: 36˝ x 29˝

Fabric and Supplies

- **Lapis:** ¾ yard for background
- **Medium green 1:** 1¾ yards (¼ yard for border, ⅜ yard for binding, and 1⅛ yards for backing)
- **Grass:** ⅓ yard for border
- **Medium green 2:** ¼ yard for border
- **Cherry:** ¾ yard for border corners and Santa's coat and hat
- **Snow:** ¾ yard for Santa's beard, eyebrows, and accents
- **Nectar 1:** ⅛ yard for stars and Santa's button
- **Nectar 2:** ¼ yard for letters
- **Ballet:** 3″ × 3″ square for Santa's lip
- **Black:** ¼ yard for Santa's mittens
- **Flesh:** ⅛ yard for Santa's face
- **Thin cotton batting:** 35″ × 42″
- **18″-wide lightweight paper-backed fusible adhesive:** 3 yards
- **12″-wide tear-away stabilizer:** 2½ yards
- **Black and gray threads for satin stitching**
- **Permanent marker**
- **Fabric pencil**

Fusible Appliqué Preparations

All appliqué pattern pieces are on pages 2, 6, and 8 of the pullout. They are printed actual size and are reversed for tracing onto fusible adhesive. Join the pieces when tracing as indicated on the pattern. Refer to Appliqué (page 7) for instructions.

Cutting Fabrics

Use a rotary cutter, mat, and ruler to cut the following pieces from the width of the fabric.

From Lapis:

Cut 1 rectangle 21½″ × 28½″ for the background.

From Medium Green 1:

Cut 4 strips 1½″ × width of fabric for the border.

Cut 1 strip 1½″ × 4½″ for the border.

Cut 4 strips 2⅛″ × width of fabric for the binding.

Use the remaining fabric for the backing 35″ × 42″.

From Grass:

Cut 4 strips 1½″ × width of fabric for the border.

Cut 1 strip 1½″ × 4½″ for the outer border.

From Medium Green 2:

Cut 4 strips 1½″ × width of fabric for the border.

From Cherry:

Cut 1 strip 4½″ × width of fabric. Subcut into 4 squares 4½″ × 4½″ for the border corners.

See appliqué instructions, page 27, to make Santa's coat (1) and hat (3A and 3B).

From Snow:

See appliqué instructions to make Santa's beard (2), eyebrows (5 and 6), and accents (9–11).

From Nectar 1:

See appliqué instructions to make Santa's button (13) and the stars (20).

From Nectar 2:

See appliqué instructions to make the letters (14–19).

From Ballet:

See appliqué instructions to make Santa's lip (7).

From Black:

See appliqué instructions to make Santa's mittens (8 and 12).

From Flesh:

See appliqué instructions to make Santa's face (4).

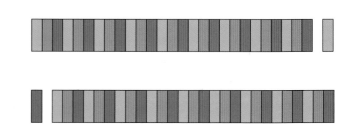

Quilt Top Assembly

Note: Assemble the quilt top before positioning and fusing the appliqués to the quilt top.

1 Sew a 1½″ × width of fabric grass strip, a 1½″ × width of fabric medium green 2 strip, and a 1½″ × width of fabric medium green 1 strip together lengthwise in the order given to make 1 border strip set. Press the seams in one direction. Repeat to make 4 border strip sets total.

2 Cut the border strip sets into 32 segments 4½″ wide for the border.

4½″

3 Sew together 7 segments 4½″ wide from Step 2 to make a side border measuring 4½″ × 21½″. Press the seams in one direction. Repeat to make 2 side borders total.

4 Sew the side borders to the 21½″ × 28½″ lapis background piece. Press the seams toward the background.

5 Sew together 9 segments 4½″ wide from Step 2 for the top border. Press. Repeat for the bottom border.

6 Sew a 1½″ × 4½″ grass piece to the medium green 1 strip at the end of one border to complete the top border. Sew a 1½″ × 4½″ medium green 1 strip to the grass strip at the end of the remaining border to complete the bottom border. Press.

7 Sew a 4½″ × 4½″ cherry square to each end of the top and bottom borders. Press the seams toward the cherry squares.

8 Sew the borders to the lapis background.

9 Referring to the quilt photo and illustration for placement, remove the paper backing from all the appliqué pieces and position them on the quilt top, overlapping pieces as necessary.

10 When you are satisfied with the placement, fuse the pieces into place, smoothing the larger pieces as you proceed.

Quilting

Refer to Layering and Quilting (page 8) and Binding (pages 8–9).

1 Sandwich the batting between the quilt top and backing, wrong sides together, smoothing the quilt top outward from the center. Baste as desired.

2 Using monofilament thread, stitch around the outside of all the satin stitched details and shapes.

3 Using a walking foot and matching thread, stitch in-the-ditch between the border and background square.

4 Bind the quilt.

Satin Stitch Appliqué

Use a tear-away stabilizer on the wrong side of the background fabric. With thread suitable for machine appliqué, satin stitch around the appliqué pieces and any detail stitching lines. To satin stitch, use a fairly narrow zigzag stitch and keep your stitch length as short as possible. Stitch over the raw edges of the fused appliqué pieces so that none of the raw edges show. Work outward from the center and smooth the fabric as you proceed.

1 Using black thread, satin stitch the face and coat details.

2 Using gray thread, straight stitch the details in Santa's beard and mustache.

3 If you like, brush a little blush onto Santa's cheeks.

4 Fill in the mouth and eyes with permanent marker.

Santa's Pet

As if the red nose weren't enough, Rudolph demands more than his fair share of attention from Santa. All the other reindeer seem to think this has gone far enough.

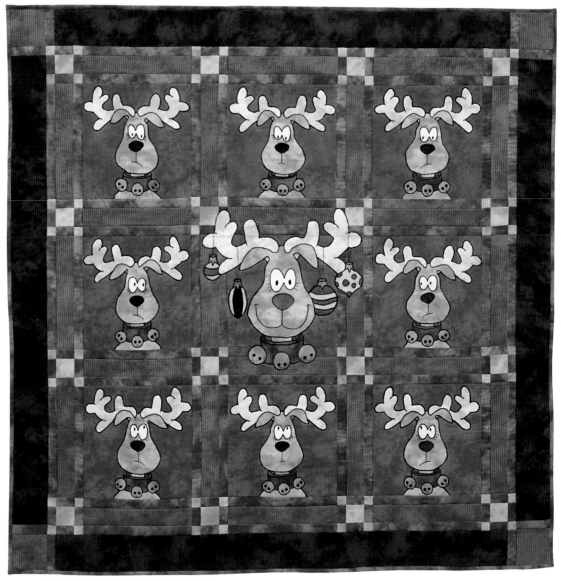

Quilt top made and quilted by: *Heidi Pridemore and The Whimsical Workshop*
Finished Quilt: 60˝ × 60˝

Fabric and Supplies

- **Indigo:** $4\frac{7}{8}$ yards ($\frac{7}{8}$ yard for outer border and 4 yards for backing)

- **Delft:** $1\frac{1}{2}$ yards for background

- **Green:** $1\frac{3}{4}$ yards ($1\frac{1}{4}$ yards for sashing and $\frac{1}{2}$ yard for binding)

- **Cherry:** 1 yard for sashing, outer-border cornerstones, reindeer's nose, and ornament

- **Butterscotch:** $\frac{7}{8}$ yard for sashing cornerstones and reindeers' heads and necks

- **Camel:** $\frac{1}{8}$ for reindeers' inner ears

- **Sand:** $\frac{3}{4}$ yard for reindeers' antlers

- **Auburn:** $\frac{1}{4}$ yard for reindeers' collars

- **Gold:** $\frac{1}{4}$ yard for collar bells and ornament tops

- **Black:** $\frac{1}{8}$ yard for reindeers' noses

- **White:** $\frac{1}{8}$ yard for reindeers' eyes

- **Purple:** $4'' \times 4''$ square for ornament

- **Sapphire:** $6'' \times 6''$ square for ornaments

- **Nectar:** fat $\frac{1}{8}$ yard for ornaments

- **Thin cotton batting:** $66'' \times 66''$

- **18″-wide lightweight paper-backed fusible adhesive:** 4 yards

- **12″-wide tear-away stabilizer:** 4 yards

- **Black thread for satin stitching**

- **Permanent marker**

- **Fabric pencil**

Fusible Appliqué Preparations

All appliqué pattern pieces are on pages 1 and 3 of the pullout. They are printed actual size and are reversed for tracing onto fusible adhesive. Join the pieces when tracing as indicated on the pattern. Refer to Appliqué (page 7) for instructions.

Cutting Fabrics

Use a rotary cutter, mat, and ruler to cut the following pieces from the width of the fabric.

From Indigo:

Cut 6 strips $4\frac{1}{2}'' \times$ width of fabric. Piece the strips together end to end as necessary and cut into 4 strips $4\frac{1}{2}'' \times 50\frac{1}{2}''$ for the outer border.

Piece the remaining fabric into a $66'' \times 66''$ square for the backing.

From Delft:

Cut 3 strips $12\frac{1}{2}'' \times$ width of fabric. Subcut into 9 squares $12\frac{1}{2}'' \times 12\frac{1}{2}''$ for the background.

From Green:

Cut 2 strips $12\frac{1}{2}'' \times$ width of fabric. Subcut into 48 strips $1\frac{1}{2}'' \times 12\frac{1}{2}''$ for the sashing.

Cut 3 strips $2\frac{1}{2}'' \times$ width of fabric. Subcut into 64 strips $1\frac{1}{2}'' \times 2\frac{1}{2}''$ for the sashing.

Cut 1 strip $1\frac{1}{2}'' \times$ width of fabric. Subcut into 8 strips $1\frac{1}{2}'' \times 4\frac{1}{2}''$ for the outer-border cornerstones.

Cut 7 strips $2\frac{1}{8}'' \times$ width of fabric for the binding.

From Cherry:

Cut 2 strips $12\frac{1}{2}'' \times$ width of fabric. Subcut into 24 strips $2\frac{1}{2}'' \times 12\frac{1}{2}''$ for the sashing.

Cut 4 squares $4\frac{1}{2}'' \times 4\frac{1}{2}''$ for the outer-border cornerstones.

See appliqué instructions, page 33, to make the large reindeer's nose (10) and the ornament (21).

From Butterscotch:

Cut 1 strip 2½″ × width of fabric. Subcut into 16 squares 2½″ × 2½″ for the sashing cornerstones.

Cut 3 strips 1½″ × width of fabric. Subcut into 64 squares 1½″ × 1½″ for the sashing cornerstones.

See appliqué instructions to make the 9 reindeers' heads and necks (4 each of 3, 4 each of 3R, 1 each of large 3).

From Camel:

See appliqué instructions to make 18 inner ears for the reindeer (4 each of 4 and 5, 4 each of 4R and 5R, 1 each of large 4 and 5).

From Sand:

See appliqué instructions to make 18 antlers for the reindeer (4 each of 1 and 2, 4 each of 1R and 2R, 1 each of large 1 and 2).

From Auburn:

See appliqué instructions to make the 9 reindeers' collars (4 each of 6 and 6R, 1 of large 6).

From Gold:

See appliqué instructions to make the 27 collar bells (4 each of 11–13, 4 each of 11R–13R, 1 each of large 11–13) and 4 ornament tops (3 of 14, 1 of 15).

From Black:

See appliqué instructions to make the 8 small reindeers' noses (4 of 10, 4 of 10R).

From Plain White:

See appliqué instructions to make 9 reindeers' eyes (4 each of 7 and 7R, 1 of large 7).

From Purple:

See appliqué instructions to make the ornament (19).

From Sapphire:

See appliqué instructions to make the ornaments (17 and 25).

From Nectar:

See appliqué instructions to make the ornaments (16, 18, 20, and 22–24).

Quilt Top Assembly

Note: Assemble and satin stitch each of the eight small reindeer on a 12½″ × 12½″ delft background square. Assemble the quilt top before positioning and finishing the large center reindeer.

1. Referring to the small reindeer A and B illustrations for placement, remove the paper backing from all the appliqué pieces for each small reindeer and position each one on a 12½″ × 12½″ delft background square, overlapping pieces as necessary. Make 8 small reindeer blocks.

Note: To make sure the direction matches the photo, do not mark or stitch the small reindeers' eyes or mouths until the quilt top is assembled.

2. When you are satisfied with the placement for each small reindeer, fuse the pieces into place, smoothing the larger pieces as you proceed.

Small reindeer A

Small reindeer B
Make all pieces reversed.

3 Referring to the satin stitch instructions on page 33, finish the raw edges of each shape.

4 Sew a 1½″ × 12½″ green strip lengthwise to each side of a 2½″ × 12½″ cherry strip to make a sashing strip. Press the seams toward the cherry strip. Repeat to make 24 sashing strips total.

Make 24.

5 Sew a 1½″ × 1½″ butterscotch square to each end of a 1½″ × 2½″ green strip to make the top row of the sashing cornerstone. Press the seams toward the green strip. Make 32 total.

Make 32.

6 Sew a 1½″ × 2½″ green strip to each side of a 2½″ × 2½″ butterscotch square to make the middle row of the sashing cornerstone. Press the seams toward the green strips. Make 16 total.

Make 16.

7 Sew 2 units from Step 5 to the top and bottom of 1 unit from Step 6 to make 1 sashing cornerstone. Make 16 total.

Make 16.

8 Starting and ending with a sashing cornerstone, sew together 4 sashing cornerstones and 3 sashing strips, alternating them to make a sashing row. Press the seams toward the sashing strips. Make 4 total.

Make 4.

9 Refer to the quilt photo and illustration for the placement of small reindeers A and B as you sew the blocks together. Starting and ending with a sashing strip, alternate 4 sashing strips and 3 small reindeer blocks to make a row. Press the seams toward the sashing strips. Make 2 rows total.

10 Repeat Step 9 with the remaining sashing strips, 2 small reindeer, and the remaining 12½″ × 12½″ delft square to make the center row. Make sure the delft square is in the middle of the pieced row. Press the seams toward the sashing strips.

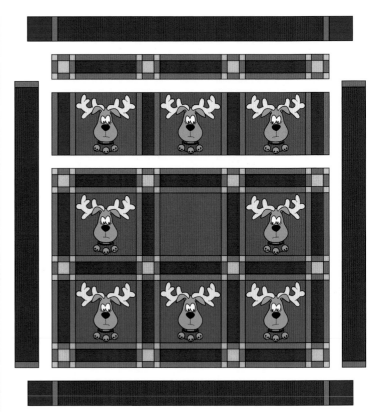

11 Referring to the quilt top layout diagram, sew the rows together to make the quilt top. Press.

12 Sew a 1½″ × 4½″ green strip to each end of the 4 indigo strips 4½″ × 50½″. Press the seams toward the green strips.

13 Sew an indigo strip to each side of the quilt top. Press the seams toward the indigo strip.

14 Sew a 4½″ × 4½″ cherry square to each end of the remaining 2 strips 4½″ × 50½″ to complete the top and bottom outer borders. Press the seams toward the green strips. Sew the borders to the quilt top. Press.

15 Referring to the large center-reindeer illustration, at right, for placement, remove the paper backing from all the appliqué pieces for the large reindeer and position them on the center indigo square, overlapping pieces as necessary.

16 When you are satisfied with the placement, fuse the pieces into place, smoothing the larger pieces as you proceed.

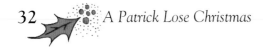

Large center reindeer

Satin Stitch Appliqué

Use a tear-away stabilizer on the wrong side of the background fabric. With thread suitable for machine appliqué, satin stitch around the appliqué pieces and any detail stitching lines. To satin stitch, use a fairly narrow zigzag stitch and keep your stitch length as short as possible. Stitch over the raw edges of the fused appliqué pieces so that none of the raw edges show. Work outward from the center and smooth the fabric as you proceed.

Using black thread, satin stitch the eyes, mouths, eyelashes, and ornament strings.

Quilting

Refer to Layering and Quilting (page 8) and Binding (pages 8–9).

1 Sandwich the batting between the quilt top and backing, wrong sides together, smoothing the quilt top outward from the center. Baste as desired.

2 Using monofilament thread, stitch around the outside of all the satin stitched details and shapes.

3 Using a walking foot and matching thread, stitch in-the-ditch between the sashing and background square and outer border.

4 Bind the quilt.

 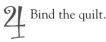

Nuts about Christmas

The crazed look on this nutcracker's face says it all!

Quilt top made and quilted by: *Heidi Pridemore and The Whimsical Workshop*
Finished Quilt: 31˝ × 45˝

Fabric and Supplies

- **Lapis:** 2¼ yards (¾ yard for background and 1½ yards for backing, and crown jewels)

- **Hunter:** ¾ yard (⅜ yard for crown top, coat and collar accents, crown jewels, and inner border and ⅜ yard for binding)

- **Cherry:** 1⅛ yards for coat, collar, accents, crown jewels, and outer border

- **Lemon:** ¼ yard for stars

- **Nectar:** ½ yard for epaulets, buttons, crown, and crown tips

- **Flesh:** ⅓ yard for face

- **Blush:** ⅛ yard for cheeks

- **Snow:** ½ yard for mustache, hair, eyebrows, and beard

- **Plain white:** fat ⅛ yard or ¼ yard for teeth and eyes

- **Thin cotton batting:** 37″ × 51″

- **18″-wide lightweight paper-backed fusible adhesive:** 3 yards

- **12″-wide tear-away stabilizer:** 3 yards

- **Bright yellow, black, and pink threads for satin stitching**

- **Permanent marker**

- **Fabric pencil**

Fusible Appliqué Preparations

All appliqué pattern pieces are on pages 3–4 of the pullout. They are printed actual size and are reversed for tracing onto fusible adhesive. Refer to Appliqué (page 7) for instructions.

Note: Cut the nectar yardage in half across the top fold. Apply fusible adhesive to the back side of one half. Set aside.

Cutting Fabrics

Use a rotary cutter, mat, and ruler to cut the following pieces from the width of the fabric.

From Lapis:

Cut 1 rectangle 21½″ × 22½″ for the background.

Cut 1 rectangle 37″ × 51″ for the backing.

See appliqué instructions, page 37, to make the crown jewels (31).

From Hunter:

Cut 4 strips 2″ × width of fabric. Subcut into 2 strips 2″ × 32½″ and 2 strips 2″ × 24½″ for the inner border.

Cut 5 strips 2⅛″ × width of fabric for the binding.

See appliqué instructions to make the coat and collar accents (3, 4, 6, and 7), crown top (13), and crown jewels (31).

From Cherry:

Cut 1 strip 10½″ × 21½″ for the coat.

Cut 2 strips 4″ × 35½″ for the side outer borders.

Cut 1 strip 4″ × 31½″ for the top outer border.

Cut 1 strip 7″ × 31½″ for the bottom outer border.

See appliqué instructions to make the collar (5), inner-border dots (30), and crown jewels (31).

From Lemon:

See appliqué instructions to make the large and small stars (23–29).

From Nectar:

See appliqué instructions to make the epaulets (1 and 2), buttons (8), crown (12), and crown tips (32).

From Flesh:

See appliqué instructions to make the face (9).

From Blush:

See appliqué instructions to make the cheeks (15).

From Snow:

See appliqué instructions to make the hair (10 and 11), mustache (16 and 17), eyebrows (20 and 21), and beard (22).

From Plain White:

See appliqué instructions to make the teeth (14) and eyes (18 and 19).

Quilt Top Assembly

Note: Do not add the bottom outer border until the satin stitching is done.

1. Referring to the quilt photo and illustration for placement, remove the paper backing from the epaulet pieces and coat trim pieces 3 and 4 and position them on the $10\frac{1}{2}'' \times 21\frac{1}{2}''$ cherry strip. Fuse into place.

2. Sew the $10\frac{1}{2}'' \times 21\frac{1}{2}''$ cherry strip to the bottom of the $21\frac{1}{2}'' \times 22\frac{1}{2}''$ lapis background piece to make the quilt top. Press the seam toward the lapis background.

3. Sew a $2'' \times 32\frac{1}{2}''$ hunter strip to each side of the quilt top. Sew a $2'' \times 24\frac{1}{2}''$ hunter strip to the top and bottom of the quilt top. Press the seams toward the strips.

4. Referring to the quilt photo, draw a light scroll line on the hunter border using a fabric pencil. (You will be satin stitching this line after the appliqué pieces are fused on.)

5. Sew a $4'' \times 35\frac{1}{2}''$ cherry outer border to each side of the quilt top. Sew a $4'' \times 31\frac{1}{2}''$ cherry outer border to the top of the quilt.

6. Using a lightbox and fabric pencil, trace the lettering on the bottom outer border. Refer to the Satin Stitch instructions on page 37, and use black thread to complete the bottom outer border. Once the stitching is complete, add the $7'' \times 31\frac{1}{2}''$ cherry outer border to the bottom of the quilt.

7. Referring to the quilt photo and illustration for placement, remove the paper backing from all the appliqué pieces and position them on the quilt top, overlapping pieces as necessary.

8. When you are satisfied with the placement, fuse the pieces into place, smoothing the larger pieces as you proceed.

Satin Stitch Appliqué

Use a tear-away stabilizer on the wrong side of the background fabric. With thread suitable for machine appliqué, satin stitch around the appliqué pieces and any detail stitching lines. To satin stitch, use a fairly narrow zigzag stitch and keep your stitch length as short as possible. Stitch over the raw edges of the fused appliqué pieces so that none of the raw edges show. Work outward from the center and smooth the fabric as you proceed.

1. Use bright yellow thread and a wide stitch (4mm–5mm wide) to satin stitch the drawn scroll.

2. Using black thread, straight stitch the details on the epaulets and teeth.

3. Using black thread, satin stitch the face details and the arms on the coat.

4. Using matching pink thread, satin stitch around the cheeks on the nutcracker's face.

Quilting

Refer to Layering and Quilting (page 8) and Binding (pages 8–9).

1. Sandwich the batting between the quilt top and backing, wrong sides together, smoothing the quilt top outward from the center. Baste as desired.

2. Using monofilament thread, stitch around the outside of all the satin stitched details and shapes.

3. Using a walking foot and matching thread, stitch in-the-ditch between the background square and the outer border.

4. Bind the quilt.

Joyride

The illustration that inspired this quilt was originally painted to become a Christmas card. From there, it went on to become the basis for a fabric collection, a cross-stitch pattern, and a rubber stamp image. I'd say that Santa's Christmas Eve trip is the epitome of a joyride!

Quilt top made and quilted by: *Heidi Pridemore and The Whimsical Workshop*
Finished Quilt: 49˝ × 42˝

Fabric and Supplies

- **Sapphire:** 3¾ yards (1 yard for background, ball, and gifts, and 2¾ yards for backing)

- **Auburn:** ⅔ yard for reindeer's body, sled, doll hair, and bear

- **Nectar:** ¾ yard for inner border and accents

- **Cherry:** 1 yard for outer border, Santa's suit, lettering, and accents

- **Green:** ¾ yard for binding and accents

- **Lemon:** ⅓ yard for stars and accents

- **Sand:** ⅓ yard for reindeer's antlers and bear accents

- **Snow:** ½ yard for Santa's coat trim, hair, and accents

- **Camel:** 6″ × 6″ square for reindeer's and bear's inner ears, and reindeer's tail

- **Purple:** ¼ yard for accents

- **Flesh:** ⅛ yard for faces of Santa, doll, and soldier and doll's arms

- **Black:** ¼ yard for accents

- **Blush:** 3″ × 3″ square for Santa's lip

- **Thin cotton batting:** 48″ × 55″

- **18″-wide lightweight paper-backed fusible adhesive:** 3½ yards

- **12″-wide tear-away stabilizer:** 5 yards

- **Black thread for satin stitching**

- **Permanent marker**

- **Fabric pencil**

Fusible Appliqué Preparations

All appliqué pattern pieces are on pages 5–6 of the pullout. They are printed actual size and are reversed for tracing onto fusible adhesive. Join the pieces when tracing as indicated on the pattern. Refer to Appliqué (page 7) for instructions.

Cutting Fabrics

Use a rotary cutter, mat, and ruler to cut the following pieces from the width of the fabric.

From Sapphire:

Cut 1 rectangle 30½″ × 37½″ for the background.

Cut and sew fabric to make 1 rectangle 48″ × 55″ for the backing.

See appliqué instructions, page 43, to make the ball (1) and gifts.

From Auburn:

See appliqué instructions for the reindeer's body (1A and 1B), the sled (1 and 2), the doll hair (3), and the bear (1).

From Nectar:

Cut 2 strips 4½″ × 38½″ and 2 strips 4½″ × 37½″ for the outer border.

See appliqué instructions to make Santa's belt buckle (17), the bells (21 and 22), the reins circles, and the soldier's epaulets (7 and 8) and coat decorations (9, 10 and 11).

From Cherry:

Cut 5 strips × width of fabric. Piece end to end as necessary and cut 2 strips 2½″ × 45½″ and 2 strips 2½″ × 42½″ for the outer border.

See appliqué instructions to make Santa's suit (2), leg (6) hat (7), arm (9), and belt loops (15 and 16); the stocking (2); the candy (2); the gifts; the ornament (2–4); the drum (1); the soldier's coat (2); the bear's bowtie (7); the reindeer's nose (6); and the lettering.

From Green:

Cut 5 strips $2\frac{1}{8}$″ × width of fabric.

See appliqué instructions to make the reins (A–I), the gifts, and Santa's mittens (11 and 12).

From Lemon:

See appliqué instructions to make the stars, gifts, and drum (2 and 3).

From Sand:

See appliqué instructions to make the antlers (2 and 3) and bear accents (2–6).

From Snow:

See appliqué instructions to make Santa's beard (3) and accents (1, 8, 10, 13, and 18), the doll's outfit (1, 10, and 11), the drum (4), the stocking (1), and the candy (1).

From Camel:

See appliqué instructions to make the reindeer's inner tail (13) and ears (4 and 5) and the bear's inner ears (8 and 9).

From Purple:

See appliqué instructions to make the ball (2 and 3), ornament (1), gifts, and doll accents (4, 5, 8, and 9).

From Flesh:

See appliqué instructions to make Santa's face (4), the doll's face and arms (2, 6, and 7), and the soldier's face (3).

From Black:

See appliqué instructions to make the soldier's accents (1 and 6) and Santa's mouth (6), belt and boots (14, 20, and 21), and the reindeer's hooves (7–10).

From Blush:

See appliqué instructions to make Santa's lip (5).

Quilt Top Assembly

Note: Assemble and satin stitch Santa, the reindeer, and the stars to the $30\frac{1}{2}$″ × $37\frac{1}{2}$″ sapphire background before adding the borders and border appliqués.

1 Referring to the quilt photo and illustration for placement, remove the paper backing from the reindeer, Santa, and the star appliqué pieces and position them on the $30\frac{1}{2}$″ × $37\frac{1}{2}$″ sapphire background piece, overlapping pieces as necessary.

2 When you are satisfied with the placement, fuse the pieces into place, smoothing the larger pieces as you proceed.

3 Sew a 4½″ × 37½″ nectar strip to the top and bottom of the sapphire background piece. Press. Sew a 4½″ × 38½″ nectar strip to each side of the sapphire background piece. Press.

4 Sew a 2½″ × 45½″ cherry strip to the top and bottom of the quilt top. Press. Sew a 2½″ × 42½″ cherry strip to each side of the quilt top. Press.

5 Referring to the quilt photo and illustrations, at right and pages 42–43, for placement, remove the paper backing from the toy appliqué pieces and position them on the quilt top, overlapping pieces as necessary.

6 When you are satisfied with the placement, fuse the pieces into place, smoothing the larger pieces as you proceed.

Gift E: Make 2, 1 as shown and 1 sapphire with lemon ribbon.

Doll

Gift B

Word

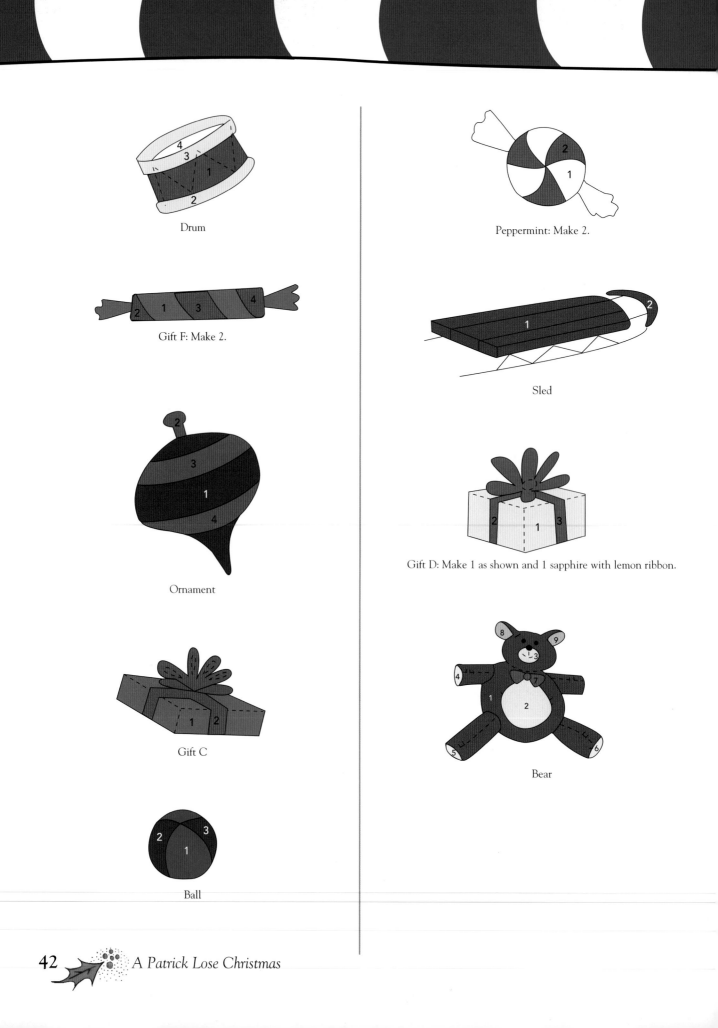

Drum

Peppermint: Make 2.

Gift F: Make 2.

Sled

Ornament

Gift D: Make 1 as shown and 1 sapphire with lemon ribbon.

Gift C

Bear

Ball

Stocking

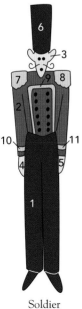

Gift A

Soldier

Satin Stitch Appliqué

Use a tear-away stabilizer on the wrong side of the background fabric. With thread suitable for machine appliqué, satin stitch around the appliqué pieces and any detail stitching lines. To satin stitch, use a fairly narrow zigzag stitch and keep your stitch length as short as possible. Stitch over the raw edges of the fused appliqué pieces so that none of the raw edges show. Work outward from the center and smooth the fabric as you proceed.

1. Using black thread, satin stitch the lettering and accents on Santa and the reindeer. Satin stitch border appliqués as shown in the quilt photo.

2. Using black thread, straight stitch the accents on the border appliqués as shown in the quilt photo.

3. Using a permanent marker, add details on the border appliqués that are too small to stitch.

4. If you like, brush a little blush onto Santa's cheeks.

Quilting

Refer to Layering and Quilting (page 8) and Binding (pages 8–9).

1. Sandwich the batting between the quilt top and backing, wrong sides together, smoothing the quilt top outward from the center. Baste as desired.

2. Using monofilament thread, stitch around the outside of all the satin stitched details and shapes.

3. Using a walking foot and matching thread, stitch in-the-ditch between the background square and outer border.

4. Using a darning foot, with the machine feed dogs lowered, stipple the background using matching thread.

5. Bind the quilt.

A Frosty Friend

*F*rom the tip of his top hat to the fringe on his scarf, this guy has holiday cheer written all over him.

Quilt top made and quilted by: *Heidi Pridemore and The Whimsical Workshop*

Finished Block: 22″ × 22″   Finished Quilt: 22″ × 30″

Fabric and Supplies

- **Hunter:** 1⅜ yards (½ yard for outer border and hat band and ⅞ yard for backing)

- **Sapphire:** ½ yard for background

- **Auburn:** ½ yard (¼ yard for inner border and sashing and ¼ yard for binding)

- **Snow:** ⅓ yard for snowman and snowflakes

- **Nectar:** ¼ yard for cornerstones and scarf

- **Cherry:** ¼ yard for scarf

- **Pumpkin:** ⅛ yard for nose

- **Black:** ¼ yard for hat, buttons, eyes, and pipe

- **Thin cotton batting:** 26″ × 34″

- **18″-wide lightweight paper-backed fusible adhesive:** 1½ yards

- **12″-wide tear-away stabilizer:** 1½ yards

- **White, black, and light gray threads for satin stitching**

- **Permanent marker**

- **Fabric pencil**

Fusible Appliqué Preparations

All appliqué pattern pieces are on pages 7–8 of the pullout. They are printed actual size and are reversed for tracing onto fusible adhesive. Refer to Appliqué (page 7) for instructions.

Cutting Fabrics

Use a rotary cutter, mat, and ruler to cut the following pieces from the width of the fabric.

From Hunter:

Cut 3 strips 4½″ × width of fabric. Subcut into 2 strips 4½″ × 20½″, 2 strips 4½″ × 12½″, and 4 squares 4½″ × 4½″ for the outer border.

Cut 1 rectangle 26″ × 34″ for the backing.

See appliqué instructions, page 47, to make the hat band (5).

From Sapphire:

Cut 1 rectangle 12½″ × 20½″ for the background.

From Auburn:

Cut 2 strips 1½″ × width of fabric. Subcut into 2 strips 1½″ × 20½″ and 2 strips 1½″ × 12½″ for the inner border.

Cut 1 strip 1½″ × width of fabric. Subcut into 8 rectangles 1½″ × 4½″ for the sashing.

Cut 4 strips 2⅛″ × width of fabric for the binding.

From Snow:

See appliqué instructions to make the snowman (1 and 2) and 17 snowflakes (21).

From Nectar:

Cut 4 squares 1½″ × 1½″ for the cornerstones.

See appliqué instructions to make the scarf (6, 10, and 14).

From Cherry:

See appliqué instructions to make the scarf strips (7–9, 11–13, and 15–17).

From Pumpkin:

See appliqué instructions to make the nose (18).

From Black:

See appliqué instructions to make the hat (3 and 4), pipe (19), eyes (20), and buttons (22, 23, 24).

Quilt Top Assembly

Note: Assemble the quilt top before positioning and fusing the appliqués to the quilt top.

1. Sew a 1½″ × 20½″ auburn strip to each side of the 12½″ × 20½″ sapphire background. Press the seams toward the strips.

2. Sew a 1½″ × 1½″ nectar square to each end of the 2 auburn strips 1½″ × 12½″. Press. Sew the 2 strips to the top and bottom of the sapphire background to make the quilt top. Press toward the inner border.

3. Sew a 1½″ × 4½″ auburn strip to each end of the 2 hunter strips 4½″ × 20½″ and sew a strip unit to each side of the quilt top. Press the seams toward the inner border.

4. Sew a 1½″ × 4½″ auburn strip to each end of the 4½″ × 12½″ hunter strips. Press the seams toward the auburn strips. Sew a 4½″ × 4½″ hunter square to each end of the strip to complete the top and bottom outer borders. Press toward the inner borders. Sew the outer borders to the quilt top. Press.

5. Referring to the quilt photo and illustration for placement, remove the paper backing from all the appliqué pieces and position them on the quilt top, overlapping pieces as necessary.

6. When you are satisfied with the placement, fuse the pieces into place, smoothing the larger pieces as you proceed.

1 Using black thread, satin stitch the mouth on the snowman.

2 Using light gray thread, straight stitch the smoke above the pipe.

3 Using white thread, satin stitch the snowflakes.

Quilting

Refer to Layering and Quilting (page 8) and Binding (pages 8–9).

1 Sandwich the batting between the quilt top and backing, wrong sides together, smoothing the quilt top outward from the center. Baste as desired.

2 Using monofilament thread, stitch around the outside of all the satin stitched details and shapes.

3 Using a walking foot and matching thread, stitch in-the-ditch between the background square and the inner border.

4 Bind the quilt.

Satin Stitch Appliqué

Use a tear-away stabilizer on the wrong side of the background fabric. With thread suitable for machine appliqué, satin stitch around the appliqué pieces and any detail stitching lines. To satin stitch, use a fairly narrow zigzag stitch and keep your stitch length as short as possible. Stitch over the raw edges of the fused appliqué pieces so that none of the raw edges show. Work outward from the center and smooth the fabric as you proceed.

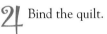

A Holiday Greeting

These characters formed the border on a fabric print from a popular group of Christmas fabrics I did years ago. I think their appeal is even stronger in this door topper, which you can use to greet your guests as they arrive for your holiday celebration. Or you can hang it above the front door, inside, to wish them a merry Christmas as they leave.

Quilt top made and quilted by: *Heidi Pridemore and The Whimsical Workshop*
Finished Quilt: 13″ × 36″

Fabric and Supplies

- **Lapis:** 1 yard (³⁄₈ yard for background and ⁵⁄₈ yard for backing)

- **Nectar:** ¼ yard for banner, snowman's scarf, reindeer's bells, and elf's accents

- **Cherry:** ½ yard (¼ yard for bottom border accent, Santa's suit and hat, candy cane, reindeer's nose, elf's hat band, and snowman's earmuffs and scarf, and ¼ yard for binding)

- **Lemon:** ⅛ yard for stars and elf's hair

- **Green:** ¼ yard for girl's mitten and hat band, reindeer's collar, and elf's outfit

- **Purple:** ¼ yard for girl's outfit and snowman's hat band

- **Auburn:** 6″ × 6″ square for girl's hair

- **Butterscotch:** 5″ × 8″ piece for reindeer

- **Flesh:** ⅛ yard for faces

- **Black:** ⅛ yard for snowman's hat and buttons and Santa's mouth

- **Blush:** ⅛ yard for cheeks and Santa's lip

- **Pumpkin:** 3″ × 6″ piece for Santa's accents and snowman's nose

- **Snow:** ⅓ yard for accents

- **Camel:** 3″ × 3″ piece for reindeer's inner ears

- **Sand:** 4″ × 8″ piece for reindeer's antlers

- **Plain white:** 4″ × 4″ square for reindeer's eyes and accent on snowman's hat

- **Thin cotton batting:** 19″ × 42″

- **18″-wide lightweight paper-backed fusible adhesive:** 2½ yards

- **12″-wide tear-away stabilizer:** 2 yards

- **Black and matching thread for satin stitching**

- **Permanent marker**

- **Fabric pencil**

- **4 curtain rings for hanging**

Fusible Appliqué Preparations

All appliqué pattern pieces are labeled Door Topper and are found on page 7 of the pullout. They are printed actual size and are reversed for tracing onto fusible adhesive. Join the pieces when tracing as indicated on the pattern. Refer to Appliqué (page 7) for instructions.

Cutting Fabrics

Use a rotary cutter, mat, and ruler to cut the following pieces from the width of the fabric.

From Lapis:

Cut 1 rectangle 11½″ × 36½″ for the background.

Cut 1 rectangle 19″ × 42″ for the backing.

From Nectar:

Cut 1 strip 2½″ × 36½″ for the bottom banner.

See appliqué instructions, page 51, to make the snowman's scarf (2, 12, and 14), reindeer's bells (7A–C), and elf's accents (7A–D and 9).

From Cherry:

Cut 3 strips 2⅛″ × width of fabric for the binding.

See appliqué instructions for Santa's suit and hat (1 and 8), the girl's candy cane stripes (12A–G), the reindeer's nose (5), the elf's hat band (5), the snowman's earmuffs (8A and 8B) and scarf stripes (13, 15 and 16), and the bottom border accent.

From Lemon:

See appliqué instructions for the stars and the elf's hair (6).

From Green:
See appliqué instructions for the girl's hat band (6) and mitten (10A–C), the reindeer's collar (6), and the elf's shirt (1) and hat (3) .

From Purple:
See appliqué instructions for the girl's jacket (1) and hat (4) and the snowman's hat band (5).

From Auburn:
See appliqué instructions for the girl's hair (7A–C).

From Butterscotch:
See appliqué instructions for the reindeer (1).

From Flesh:
See appliqué instructions for Santa's face (4), the girl's face (3), and the elf's face (4).

From Black:
See appliqué instructions for the snowman's hat (4 and 6) and buttons (11A and 11B) and Santa's mouth (5).

From Blush:
See appliqué instructions for the girl's cheeks (8A and 8B), Santa's lip (6) and cheeks (7A and 7B), the elf's cheeks (8A and 8B), and the snowman's cheeks (10A and 10B).

From Pumpkin:
See appliqué instructions for Santa's coat accents (3A and 3B) and hat accent (9) and the snowman's nose (9).

From Snow:
See appliqué instructions for the girl's candy cane (11A and 11B), collar (2), pom-pom (5), and cuff (9); Santa's beard, mustache, coat trim, and hat trim (2); the elf's collar (2); and the snowman (1 and 3).

From Camel:
See appliqué instructions for the reindeer's inner ears (3A and 3B).

From Sand:
See appliqué instructions for the reindeer's antlers (2A and 2B).

From Plain White:
See appliqué instructions for the reindeer's eyes (4) and the snowman's hat accent (7).

Quilt Top Assembly
Note: Position and fuse the appliqués before assembling the quilt top.

1. Referring to the quilt photo and illustrations for placement, remove the paper backing from all the appliqué pieces and position them on the 11½″ × 36½″ lapis background, overlapping pieces as necessary. Position the accent piece on the 2½″ × 36½″ nectar bottom banner.

2. When you are satisfied with the placement, fuse the pieces into place, smoothing the larger pieces as you proceed.

3. Sew the nectar strip to the bottom of the lapis rectangle to make the background. Press the seam toward the nectar strip.

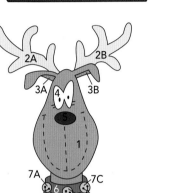

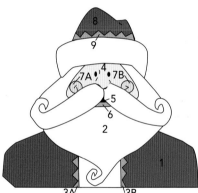

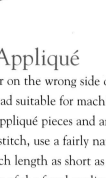

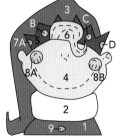

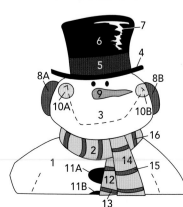

Satin Stitch Appliqué

Use a tear-away stabilizer on the wrong side of the background fabric. With thread suitable for machine appliqué, satin stitch around the appliqué pieces and any detail stitching lines. To satin stitch, use a fairly narrow zigzag stitch and keep your stitch length as short as possible. Stitch over the raw edges of the fused appliqué pieces so that none of the raw edges show. Work outward from the center and smooth the fabric as you proceed.

Using black thread, satin stitch the details on the snowman, the elf, Santa, the reindeer, and the girl. Satin stitch the lettering on the bottom banner.

Quilting

Refer to Layering and Quilting (page 8) and Binding (pages 8–9).

1 Sandwich the batting between the quilt top and backing, wrong sides together, smoothing the quilt top outward from the center. Baste as desired.

2 Using monofilament thread, stitch around the outside of all the satin stitched details and shapes.

3 Using a walking foot and matching thread, stitch in-the-ditch between the background rectangle and bottom banner.

4 Use the arch template on page 8 of the pullout and trace the arch across the top of the quilt. Trim the quilt along the arch to make the curved top on the door topper.

5 Bind the door topper.

6 Space curtain rings evenly across the back of the banner so they are hidden slightly below the top of the banner; hand stitch the rings in place.

A Holiday Greeting **51**

Christmas Collage

Here's a collection of pillows to add a touch
of the holiday spirit throughout your home.

Reindeer Pillow

Pillow made by: Heidi Pridemore and The Whimsical Workshop Finished Pillow: 24″ × 24″ square

Fabric and Supplies

- **Nectar:** 3/8 yard for ornaments and piping

- **Green:** 1 1/4 yards (1/2 yard for outer border and reindeer's collar and 3/4 yard for backing)

- **Delft:** fat 1/4 yard (or 1/2 yard) for background

- **Cherry:** 1/4 yard for checkerboard border, ornament, and reindeer's nose

- **Gold:** 8″ × 8″ square for ornament tops and bells

- **Snow:** 1/4 yard for checkerboard border

- **Butterscotch:** 1/4 yard for reindeer's head and neck

- **Plain white:** 4″ × 4″ square for reindeer's eyes

- **Sand:** fat 1/8 yard (or 1/4 yard) for reindeer's antlers

- **Lapis:** 6″ × 6″ square for ornaments

- **Camel:** 3″ × 3″ square for reindeer's inner ear

- **Purple:** 6″ × 6″ square for ornament

- **18″-wide lightweight paper-backed fusible adhesive:** 1 yard

- **12″-wide tear-away stabilizer:** 1 yard

- **1/4″ cording for pillow piping:** 3 1/4 yards

- **Black thread for satin stitching**

- **Permanent marker**

- **Fabric pencil**

- **24″ × 24″ pillow form**

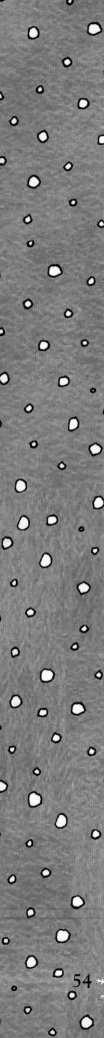

Fusible Appliqué Preparations

All appliqué pattern pieces are on pages 1 and 3 of the pullout. Be sure to use the large reindeer, collar, and bell pieces 1–11. Refer to Appliqué (page 7) for instructions.

Cutting Fabrics

Use a rotary cutter, mat, and ruler to cut the following pieces from the width of the fabric.

From Nectar:

Cut 3 strips 2″ × width of fabric for the piping.

See appliqué instructions, page 55, for the ornaments (16, 18, 20, and 22–24).

From Green:

Cut 2 strips 2½″ × 20½″ and 2 strips 2½″ × 24½″ for the outer border.

Cut 2 strips 16½″ × 24½″ for each pillow back half.

See appliqué instructions for the reindeer's collar (6).

From Delft:

Cut 1 square 16½″ × 16½″ for the background.

From Cherry:

Cut 2 strips 2½″ × width of fabric. Subcut into 18 squares 2½″ × 2½″ for the checkerboard border.

See appliqué instructions for the reindeer's nose (10) and the ornament (21).

From Gold:

See appliqué instructions for the ornament tops (14 and 15) and bells (11–13).

From Snow:

Cut 2 strips 2½″ × width of fabric. Subcut into 18 squares 2½″ × 2½″ for the checkerboard border.

From Butterscotch:

See appliqué instructions for the reindeer's head and neck (3).

From Plain White:

See appliqué instructions for the reindeer's eyes (7).

From Sand:

See appliqué instructions for the antlers (1 and 2).

From Lapis:

See appliqué instructions for the ornaments (17 and 25).

From Camel:

See appliqué instructions for the reindeer's inner ears (4 and 5).

From Purple:

See appliqué instructions for the ornament (19).

Pillow Top Assembly

Note: Assemble the pillow top before positioning and fusing the appliqués to the pillow top.

1. Starting with a 2½″ × 2½″ cherry square, sew together 4 cherry squares and 4 snow squares, alternating them to make the side border. Press the seams toward the cherry squares. Repeat to make 2 side borders total.

2. Sew the side borders to the 16½″ × 16½″ background square. Press the seams toward the background.

3. Starting with a 2½″ × 2½″ cherry square, sew together 5 cherry squares and 5 snow squares to make the top border. Press the seams toward the cherry squares. Repeat to make the bottom border.

4 Sew the top and bottom borders to the background square to make the pillow top. Press the seams toward the background.

5 Sew a 2½″ × 20½″ green strip to each side of the pillow top. Press the seams toward the green strips. Sew a 2½″ × 24½″ green strip to the top and bottom of the pillow top. Press.

6 Referring to the photo on page 53 and illustrations below and on page 33 for placement, remove the paper backing from all the appliqué pieces and position them on the quilt top, overlapping pieces as necessary.

7 When you are satisfied with the placement, fuse the pieces into place, smoothing the larger pieces as you proceed.

Satin Stitch Appliqué

Use a tear-away stabilizer on the wrong side of the background fabric. With thread suitable for machine appliqué, satin stitch around the appliqué pieces and any detail stitching lines. To satin stitch, use a fairly narrow zigzag stitch and keep your stitch length as short as possible. Stitch over the raw edges of the fused appliqué pieces so that none of the raw edges show. Work outward from the center and smooth the fabric as you proceed.

1 Using black thread, satin stitch the details on the reindeer's face and the bells.

2 Using black thread, straight stitch the ornament strings.

Pillow Assembly

1 Sew the 2″ × width of fabric nectar strips together end to end, using diagonal seams to make a 2″ × 115″ strip. Refer to Binding, Step 2, on page 8.

2 Fold over the beginning of the nectar strip ½″ and press to create a finished end. Fold the strip in half lengthwise, wrong sides together, and press. Starting 1″ away from the folded finished end, insert the ¼″ cording in the middle of the folded strip.

3 Using matching thread and a zipper foot, stitch down the length of the strip, with the stitching tight against the cording. Trim the seam allowance to ¼″.

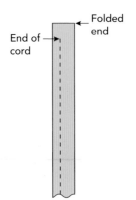

End of cord

Folded end

4 Leaving about 2″ of the finished end free and beginning at the center of one side of the pillow, pin the piping in place around the pillow, matching the raw edges. The piping will curve slightly around each corner. Clip the piping seam allowance at the corners. Using a zipper foot, sew the piping to the pillow top on top of the previous stitching.

5 When you reach a position about 3″ from the start of the stitching, line up the end of the piping with the starting point of the cording. Trim the end of the piping flush with the starting end of the cording. Tuck the end of the piping into the middle of the 2″ of free end so the cording ends are flush. Continue to stitch the piping in place until it is completely attached.

Trim the top piece here and tuck into the bottom piece.

Clip corner.

6 Fold ¼″ over on one long edge of each 16½″ × 24½″ pillow back half and press. Fold over another ¼″ and press again. Sew the folded edge down to finish one edge of each pillow back half.

7 Place both pillow back halves on top of the pillow top, right sides together, matching the raw edges and overlapping the finished edges of the pillow back halves.

8 Using a zipper foot, sew together the pillow top, piping, and pillow back halves to complete the Reindeer Pillow.

9 Turn the Reindeer Pillow right side out and insert the 24″ × 24″ pillow form.

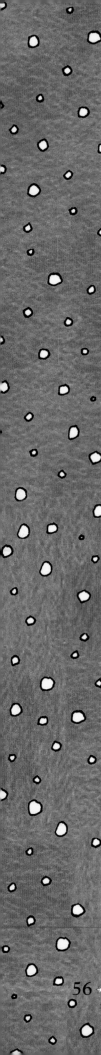

A Patrick Lose Christmas

Gift Pillow

Pillow made by: Heidi Pridemore and The Whimsical Workshop   Finished Pillow: 18˝ × 18˝ square

Fabric and Supplies

- **Nectar:** ½ yard for piping and bow
- **Green:** ¼ yard for checkerboard border and leaves
- **Delft:** fat ¼ yard (or ⅓ yard) for background
- **Cherry:** 1 yard (½ yard for outer border, gift, and berries and ½ yard for backing)
- **Snow:** ¼ yard for checkerboard border
- **18˝-wide lightweight paper-backed fusible adhesive:** ¾ yard

- **12˝-wide tear-away stabilizer:** ⅝ yard
- **¼˝ cording for pillow piping:** 2¼ yards
- **Black thread for satin stitching**
- **Permanent marker**
- **Fabric pencil**
- **18˝ × 18˝ pillow form**

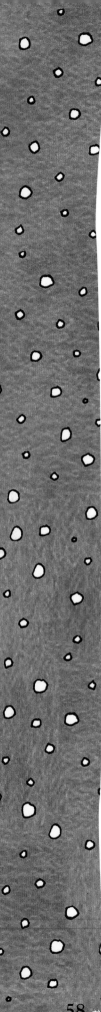

Fusible Appliqué Preparations

All appliqué pattern pieces are on page 8 of the pullout. They are printed actual size and are reversed for tracing onto fusible adhesive. Refer to Appliqué (page 7) for instructions.

Cutting Fabrics

Use a rotary cutter, mat, and ruler to cut the following pieces from the width of the fabric.

From Nectar:

Cut 2 strips 2″ × width of fabric for the piping.

See appliqué instructions, page 59, for the bow (2, 3, 4, and 5).

From Green:

Cut 1 strip $2\frac{1}{2}″$ × width of fabric. Subcut into 12 squares $2\frac{1}{2}″ × 2\frac{1}{2}″$ for the checkerboard border.

See appliqué instructions for the leaves (6 and 7).

From Delft:

Cut 1 square $10\frac{1}{2}″ × 10\frac{1}{2}″$ for the background square.

From Cherry:

Cut 2 strips $2\frac{1}{2}″$ × width of fabric. Subcut into 2 strips $2\frac{1}{2}″ × 18\frac{1}{2}″$ and 2 strips $2\frac{1}{2}″ × 14\frac{1}{2}″$ for the outer border.

Cut 2 strips $13\frac{1}{2}″ × 18\frac{1}{2}″$ for the pillow back halves.

See appliqué instructions for the gift (1) and berries (8, 9, and 10).

From Snow:

Cut 1 strip $2\frac{1}{2}″$ × width of fabric. Subcut into 12 squares $2\frac{1}{2}″ × 2\frac{1}{2}″$ for the checkerboard border.

Pillow Top Assembly

Note: Assemble the pillow top before positioning and fusing the appliqués to the pillow top.

1. Starting with a $2\frac{1}{2}″ × 2\frac{1}{2}″$ snow square, sew together 3 snow squares and 2 green squares, alternating them to make the side border. Press the seams toward the green squares. Repeat to make 2 side borders total.

2. Sew the side borders to the $10\frac{1}{2}″ × 10\frac{1}{2}″$ background square. Press the seams toward the background.

3. Starting with a $2\frac{1}{2}″ × 2\frac{1}{2}″$ green square, sew together 4 green squares and 3 snow squares to make the top border. Press the seams toward the green squares. Repeat to make the bottom border.

4. Sew the top and bottom borders to the background square to make the pillow top. Press the seams toward the background.

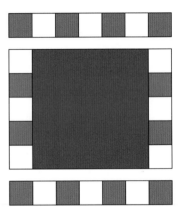

5. Sew a $2\frac{1}{2}″ × 14\frac{1}{2}″$ cherry strip to each side of the pillow top. Press the seams toward the cherry strips. Sew a $2\frac{1}{2}″ × 18\frac{1}{2}″$ cherry strip to the top and bottom of the pillow top. Press.

6 Referring to the pillow photo and illustration for placement, remove the paper backing from all the appliqué pieces and position them on the quilt top, overlapping pieces as necessary.

7 When you are satisfied with the placement, fuse the pieces into place, smoothing the larger pieces as you proceed.

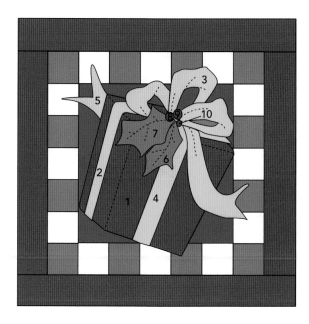

Satin Stitch Appliqué

Use a tear-away stabilizer on the wrong side of the background fabric. With thread suitable for machine appliqué, satin stitch around the appliqué pieces and any detail stitching lines. To satin stitch, use a fairly narrow zigzag stitch and keep your stitch length as short as possible. Stitch over the raw edges of the fused appliqué pieces so that none of the raw edges show. Work outward from the center and smooth the fabric as you proceed.

Using black thread, straight stitch the vines on the leaves and the bows.

Pillow Assembly

1 Sew the 2″ × width of fabric nectar strips together end to end, using diagonal seams to make a 2″ × 80″ strip. Refer to Binding, Step 2, on page 8.

2 Refer to Steps 2–5 on page 56 to sew the piping to the pillow top.

3 Fold ¼″ over on one long edge of each 13½″ × 18½″ pillow back half and press. Fold over another ¼″ and press again. Sew the folded edge down to finish one edge of each pillow back half.

4 Place both pillow back halves on top of the pillow top, right sides together, matching the raw edges and overlapping the finished edges of the pillow back halves.

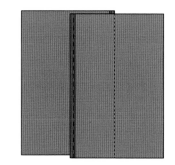

5 Using a zipper foot, sew together the pillow top, piping, and pillow back halves to complete the Gift Pillow.

6 Turn the Gift Pillow right side out and insert the 18″ × 18″ pillow form.

Christmas Tree Pillow

Pillow made by: *Heidi Pridemore and The Whimsical Workshop*   Finished Pillow: 12″ × 16″

Fabric and Supplies

- **Nectar:** ¼ yard for piping, star, and lights

- **Green:** ¾ yard (⅜ yard for outer border and tree and ⅜ yard for backing)

- **Delft:** fat ⅛ yard (or ¼ yard) for background

- **Cherry:** ⅛ yard for checkerboard border and lights

- **Snow:** ⅛ yard for checkerboard border

- **Lapis:** 4″ × 4″ square for lights

- **Purple:** 4″ × 4″ square for lights

- **Pumpkin:** 4″ × 4″ square for lights

- **18″-wide lightweight paper-backed fusible adhesive:** ½ yard

- **12″-wide tear-away stabilizer:** ½ yard

- **¼″ cording for pillow piping:** 2 yards

- **Black thread for satin stitching**

- **Permanent marker**

- **Fabric pencil**

- **12″ × 16″ pillow form**

Fusible Appliqué Preparations

All appliqué pattern pieces are on page 1 of the pullout. They are printed actual size and are reversed for tracing onto fusible adhesive. Join the pieces when tracing as indicated on the pattern. Refer to Appliqué (page 7) for instructions.

Cutting Fabrics

Use a rotary cutter, mat, and ruler to cut the following pieces from the width of the fabric.

From Nectar:

Cut 2 strips 2″ × width of fabric for the piping.

See appliqué instructions, page 62, for the star (5) and lights (6).

From Green:

Cut 4 strips 2½″ × 12½″ for the outer border.

Cut 2 strips 9½″ × 16½″ for the pillow back halves.

See appliqué instructions for the tree (1–4).

From Delft:

Cut 1 rectangle 6½″ × 9½″ for the background.

From Cherry:

Cut 1 strip 2″ × width of fabric. Subcut into 12 squares 2″ × 2″ for the checkerboard border.

See appliqué instructions for the lights (6).

From Snow:

Cut 1 strip 2″ × width of fabric. Subcut into 12 squares 2″ × 2″ for the checkerboard border.

From Lapis:

See appliqué instructions for the lights (6).

From Purple:

See appliqué instructions for the lights (6).

From Pumpkin:

See appliqué instructions for the lights (6).

Pillow Top Assembly

Note: Assemble the pillow top before positioning and fusing the appliqués to the pillow top.

1. Starting with a 2″ × 2″ snow square, sew together 3 snow squares and 3 cherry squares, alternating them to make the side border. Press the seams toward the cherry squares. Repeat to make a second side border and top and bottom borders.

2. Sew the side borders to the 6½″ × 9½″ background. Press the seams toward the background.

3. Sew the top and bottom borders to the background to make the pillow top. Press the seams toward the background.

4. Sew a 2″ × 12½″ green strip to each side of the pillow top. Press the seams toward the green strips. Sew a 2½″ × 12½″ green strip to the top and bottom of the pillow top. Press.

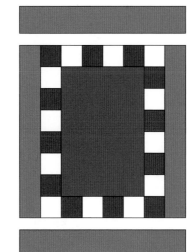

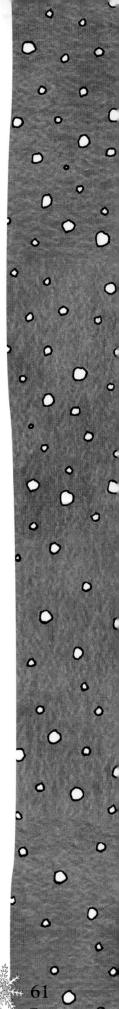

Christmas Collage   61

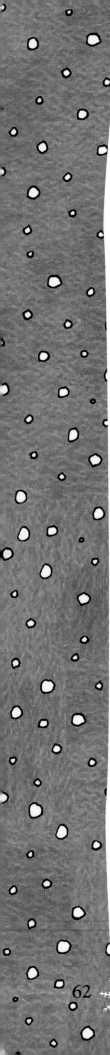

5 Referring to the pillow photo and illustration for placement, remove the paper backing from all the appliqué pieces and position them on the quilt top, overlapping pieces as necessary.

6 When you are satisfied with the placement, fuse the pieces into place, smoothing the larger pieces as you proceed.

Satin Stitch Appliqué

Use a tear-away stabilizer on the wrong side of the background fabric. With thread suitable for machine appliqué, satin stitch around the appliqué pieces and any detail stitching lines. To satin stitch, use a fairly narrow zigzag stitch and keep your stitch length as short as possible. Stitch over the raw edges of the fused appliqué pieces so that none of the raw edges show. Work outward from the center and smooth the fabric as you proceed.

Using black thread, satin stitch the details on the tree.

Pillow Assembly

1 Sew the 2″ × width of fabric nectar strips together end to end using diagonal seams to make a 2″ × 72″ strip. Refer to Binding, Step 2, on page 8.

2 Refer to Steps 2–5 on page 56 to sew the piping to the pillow top.

3 Fold ¼″ over on one long edge of each 9½″ × 16½″ pillow back half and press. Fold over another ¼″ and press again. Sew the folded edge down to finish one edge of each pillow back half.

4 Place both pillow back halves on top of the pillow top, right sides together, matching the raw edges and overlapping the finished edges of the pillow back halves.

5 Using a zipper foot, sew together the pillow top, piping, and pillow back halves to complete the Christmas Tree Pillow.

6 Turn the Christmas Tree Pillow right side out and insert the 12″ × 16″ pillow form.

Sources

For a list of other fine books from C&T Publishing, ask for a free catalog:

C&T Publishing, Inc.
P.O. Box 1456
Lafayette, CA 94549

(800) 284-1114

Email: ctinfo@ctpub.com
Website: www.ctpub.com

C&T Publishing's professional photography services are now available to the public. Visit us at www.ctmediaservices.com.

For quilting supplies:

The Cotton Patch
1025 Brown Ave.
Lafayette, CA 94549

(800) 835-4418 or
(925) 283-7883

Email: CottonPa@aol.com
Website: www.quiltusa.com

Note: Fabrics used in the quilts shown may not be currently available, as fabric manufacturers keep most fabrics in print for only a short time.

About the Author

Patrick has spent his professional years in a variety of creative fields. He began his career as an actor and singer, which eventually led him to designing costumes for stage and screen. Costuming credits include more than 50 productions and work with celebrities such as Liza Minnelli and Jane Seymour.

An artist and illustrator since childhood, Patrick works in many mediums. When he sits down to "doodle" at the drawing board, he never knows what one of his designs might become. But, whether it's designing quilts, wearable art, stationery products, or home decor, he enjoys creating it all.

He is probably most well known for his very successful and long-running collections of fabric from Timeless Treasures and Moda that include his trademark marbleized solids, which are trendsetters in the industry. Patrick's quilts, crafts, clothing, and home decorating accessories have appeared in such distinguished magazines as *Better Homes & Gardens*, *American Patchwork and Quilting*, *Country Crafts*, *Christmas Ideas*, *Halloween Tricks & Treats*, and many more. He has also written books on quilting and crafting for C&T Publishing and Sterling Publishing and has appeared on several television programs, including *The Carol Duvall Show*, *Simply Quilts*, *America Sews*, and *Martha's Sewing Room*.

Patrick invites you to visit his website at www.patricklose.net to see what's new. You can also email him at patricklose@gmail.com.

Great Titles

from C&T PUBLISHING

fast fun & easy CHRISTMAS STOCKINGS
Susan S. Terry
Festive Fabric Projects to Stir Your Imagination

gift box studio
GIFT BOXES • CARDS • EMBELLISHMENTS
HOLIDAY

A Laurel Burch CHRISTMAS
Color the Season Beautiful with 25 Quilts & Crafts

fast fun & easy CHRISTMAS DECORATIONS
Linda Johansen
Festive Fabric Keepsakes to Create & Embellish

CREATE & TREASURE from C&T Publishing
READY-TO-GO! BLANK BOARD BOOK
3-D STAR
8" × 6½"
• Acid Free
• No Prep
• Bonus Idea Brochure
• Fun and Easy to Decorate
• Make One Tonight
CAN $8.95 / US $7.95
ISBN 978-1-57120-555-7

A Cozy QUILTED CHRISTMAS
90 Designs, 17 Projects to Decorate Your Home
Kim Schaefer